Understand Me

Spencer Stott

Introduction

Let me introduce myself before I tell you the whole story.

I am Spencer.

I am 9 years old.

I have a kind of autism known as Asperger syndrome. I also have PDA which stands for Pathological Demand Avoidance. I was diagnosed when I was around seven years old, I will go into more detail as the book goes along about how mum actually made me not even realise that I was getting a diagnosis. I thought at the age of seven that I had a super brain. That was what mum told me and that's why we had all these different appointments. She wasn't wrong either. I still do have a super brain and I wouldn't want to change for anyone!

My autism is just me. I'm no different than anyone else although I was made to feel that way at the beginning. I struggle with people getting close to me. No-one really cuddles me apart from my mum and dad on a good day but even then, I'm not fussed on hugs. The only person that can hug me is my dog, Connie.

Teeth brushing is disgusting. The toothpaste is too soft, and I can't stand the texture in my mouth although I have found a way to cope with that. Mum says it's one demand that I need to do or when I get older, I am going to be in the dentist chair a lot. If you are anything like me and find teeth brushing the worst task of the day, there is one way that will keep your mum sweet. Just brush them a tiny bit but then spit it out and repeat. That way, your teeth have been brushed and you keep your mum happy.

I hate demands. Sometimes I can live with it because that's life, but if it's a teacher or when I am in a rush it makes me feel sick. Mum says that when I feel sick it means I am anxious.

I live and breathe anything to do with technology. Maybe I got that from my dad. He works with computers as his job. I love coding and at my most recent school, I was given the role of digital leader. That was pretty cool. I get to go to different schools and talk about internet safety. I also speak to the older people who don't understand computers and help them.

Since mum found out about my PDA she started to speak to me a little better. She gave me more choices instead of just telling me what to do. It helps when people give you choices as things seem calmer then.

As you will find out in the book. I hate anyone talking like they're in charge or when people are bossy. I found teachers do this a LOT! That's when I don't get on with them. It's a shame because if everyone spoke to each other kindly we would get a lot further in life and lots more would be done.

Sometimes I struggle with the way people talk to me. I still find this a little bit confusing if mum and dad are upset with me, they raise their voice. I see this as shouting, but they always say that they aren't shouting. This doesn't happen often though because mum and dad are pretty cool, and they've figured out how to get the best out of me which is not to rush me. If everything is relaxed, then I am relaxed, although mum does look stressed most school mornings running around like a headless chicken. A headless chicken? Ok so if you're like me you're thinking my mum is running around with a headless chicken? Haha, no - I don't mean that I just mean mum seems in one big rush, but then she tells me we aren't in a rush and everything is fine. How confusing is that?

I am not a big fan of praise. If my mum is happy with something and praises me, I say that's cool but if a teacher was to tell me I was good at something in front of some different adults I would roll my eyes. I hate it. In fact, now at school, my teacher does "opposites" with me. It may sound confusing but if she says I did a rubbish piece of writing that means it's good. I guess I can be difficult to understand sometimes.

I think you've heard enough about me. I am a happy kid now, but I wasn't in my younger days. Things were tough but I got through it. Make yourself comfy and remember - things might seem sad at the beginning but they do get better.

Chapter 1 – The Beginning

This is the hard part, the worst part - which is the beginning. It's a shame that we can't make the book start on a happy part, but we have to start at the difficult part so it's in the right order. Things always need to be in the right order.

It makes me feel sad thinking back, but I am hoping that this book will help you know that things can get better, so long as you are understood. Being understood is the difficult bit.

Primary school reception year - how would I describe it? I know I was looking forward to starting school for the first time. Mum said that my first week went well. The new teacher even said that I wasn't having any problems and I was one of the children that seemed confident and happy. The new teacher, she seemed nice for the first week but after that, I have to admit she seemed to look at me strangely. Her eyebrows always raised at me and I was unsure why or what I was doing wrong. I didn't quite understand the way she looked at me? I wasn't sure if she had eaten something sour - like a sour Haribo or whether this was just her facial expression. Her Haribo face never disappeared all year.

The reception classroom was split up into sections, one being the sandpit area, the other being the water area (which was a large plastic container with fake boats floated around). Next was the painting area alongside the aprons hung up for you to change into. The painting area only meant one thing – it was one of those areas where you were going to get messy. I hated getting messy hands.

Next was the music area. I hated it. A bunch of kids banging tambourines and making a racket wasn't my idea of fun. The noise hurt my ears. Then standing in the corner was a pretend shop filled with pretend cartons of beans and cutlery and pots and pans. I couldn't quite understand the shop either, it was obvious that it was all fake and it seemed a waste of time.

My favourite part was the construction area. This had building blocks in with Lego. I understood Lego and blocks from home. I could sit there for hours. I understood the blocks. When I was at home, I would use my blocks and create structures with all the blocks attached to each other. I was in a happy place playing here and using my imagination. It felt more real than the pretend shop and made sense to me.

CLAP CLAP! Went the teacher's hands. She would tell us to move around into the next section. I didn't want to go where my hands felt awful and messy. I hated the feeling. I also didn't want to go close to the music area as it hurt my ears too much. I didn't know how to explain to the teacher back then. I didn't know what I know now which was the simple fact that it was all too much sensory overload on me. I guess she didn't know either, or just thought that I was being stubborn by not wanting to move.

I could feel her hand go inside my neck collar as she tried to move me. This was a bad move; I remember getting that upset one time I was led to the corridor with the teacher looking at me strangely. She dumped me just outside the classroom door and glared down at me. This made me feel angry. Before I knew what I was doing, I tore down the posters in the hallway and tried ripping my clothes. I couldn't understand why the teacher needed me to do all the things that I struggled with. The teachers were shocked. They called mum and explained to her that I had been naughty.

This wasn't the first time that they told mum things. Probably every day after that when the school bell rang, they would tell mum to come inside and talk with her as something had happened.

As the children hurried to the cloakroom to grab their coats and bags, I would be told to wait on my chair. I could see my mum had arrived first on the playground, but we seemed always the last to leave. It became a regular thing. Mum sitting down next to me on the small chairs near my school desk with the teacher explaining what had gone wrong. The teacher never spoke about what went right that day, but there were so many things that I did do that were right. Maybe if the teachers focused on all the positive things that I could do, then maybe things would have been different.

Each day there was a problem, I wasn't sitting on the carpet still, I wasn't looking at the teacher when it was storytime, I was eating my pack lunch too slow ... the list goes on, you get the idea.

Reception was tough! Not only was I struggling with all the demands placed on me and especially having to do activities that I hated the feel of, but I was also feeling poorly all the time. I had cold after cold after cold. I always kept getting ear infections. Mum said that I was having off days because I wasn't feeling well, I agreed. We went to the doctors who told me that I had sticky ear. I felt my ear, it wasn't sticky, but mum said it was something to do with the inside of my ear. We had to go to the hospital and get grommets fitted. Once we had this out of the way I would feel so much better and school would be a little easier.

Soon after the hospital trip and returning to school I think I had a good week. Mum told me that it must have been my ear that was irritating me for so long. But things didn't change, I still felt like the scatty teacher was the same. That she was still trying to ruin my day.

The school line in the morning was difficult. The other children thought it was funny to bang into each other and not line up properly. Me and mum would always be the first on the playground, so I always tried to get the front spot to avoid getting pushed. I didn't like being pushed and now I understand that was part of my autism. In fact, I hated being touched or grabbed. It hurt, but other people didn't understand this. They found it funny, which made me angry.

This was just the start of my day.

Chapter 2 - Year 1

A new year and a new teacher. I needed this next step as I didn't like being in trouble all the time and I was unsure why it kept happening to me? The summer holidays were good. Mum was relaxed and happy we both had a positive feeling. A feeling that this new year away from the scatty teacher would work out well. I was finally free from sour Haribo face.

My classroom was different this time, but it felt better. We had desks and fewer toys, less messy things that I would have been forced to take part in. I wanted to learn, I still do now ... I am always interested in learning and always want to do my best.

Back in year one. I was happy to learn, and the new teacher seemed nice. Then again, they always seem nice to start with but then things change. For the first term, I was doing good. I enjoyed reading and learning about real things like numbers. The classroom was going well but I was still finding things tricky.

Playtimes were the worst. I wanted to play football with the other boys but when I got kicked with the ball I would cry. It really hurt when the boys wouldn't let me play. I asked why and they told me that I was a really bad player so I wasn't allowed to join in. This made me sad, but then it would make me angry. I would storm off with an angry face, trying not to cry.

Lunchtimes were hard. The dining hall was busy, and things got complicated, there was a colour code for food. Mum would have to pick my food in advance and the coloured band I had to wear would indicate what meals my mum had chosen.

How crazy is that?

Some days I didn't want to wear a red band and wanted to wear yellow, but the dinner lady told me that I had to wear the colour band that mum had selected. At the time I didn't understand that the band represented the meal. All I knew was that certain days I wanted a different colour and I didn't care about the meal, but no one was listening to me so I would get angry. I was confused, the school was making things complicated even more. Looking back at it now why couldn't things be a little more simpler and the dinner lady could just understand that this was causing me to get upset, why couldn't they be handed a sheet of paper that had my food choices on and allow me to wear whatever band I wanted. The whole band thing was stupid in my eyes.

As for lunch, mum decided that maybe it would be a better idea to take a packed lunch. At least I knew what I was going to eat and there was no messing around wearing different coloured bands. We started packed lunches, but another crazy rule was that people who ate a packed lunch had to sit in a different place to those who had school dinners. This meant I had to sit on a long table with all the kids that had packed lunches. I found this tricky. The strong smell of their juice was making me gag. I also had a thing about anything creamy. The kids that were eating yoghurts would tease me and try and push it under my nose. At this point, I got really mad. I would kick the chairs in front of me and without thinking I would hurt another student. I don't like to think of that now, but it is what happened and back then I didn't know how to control my emotions. It wasn't right that the kids teased me like that though. So, as you can imagine I got red face slips to bring home to show my mum. The slips of paper were to show my mum how I had been behaving that day. Red faces for bad behaviour, green faces for good behaviour.

The playground became a sad place for me, from being marched out of the dining hall to being chucked out onto the cold playground and walking around on my own. I would show an angry face. Kids started to become scared of me, but I think they liked my reaction. The teachers then decided that I needed an area of my own where I could play with some blocks in the playground. This made me a little happier at the time as I had my own little space. It had its benefits - it had a cover from the rain and I was allowed to let people in if I wanted them to join me so it was pretty much on my terms. Now I think back it was pretty bad that I had to have a section to myself. It feels like they treated me like an animal in a zoo. Why couldn't I just join in and be like the others? Why was I made to feel so different?

Assemblies were the next mission! I found them boring. I was pretty vocal about that point too. I would shout out and let them know how boring it was. The teachers didn't like my honesty and often ushered me out. Most of the kids got certificates whilst I got nothing, it made me feel sad that the other children were getting rewarded and I hardly ever did. The other children were often nasty to me and would snigger and point. This again made me angry so guess what? I would be marched out of the assembly hall and taken to an area outside of the classroom to sit and wait for the assembly to be over. You get the picture - there were lots of angry moments. Me and assemblies just didn't work well.

Most evenings after school I had to give mum a slip of paper. It had a red sad face, a face with no expression, and then a green happy face. Most nights after the long talk in the classroom with the teacher, me and mum we would walk back to the car with the sad face ticked on my slip. We got in the car and mum would start crying. She asked me a few times "Why do I keep having bad days?" She just wanted me to be good or have at least one good day. I tried hard to do this, but it just never happened. I didn't want to be naughty, I wanted to be happy. No one understood - not even my mum and dad back then. School was hard.

Fast forward a few weeks and I'm sitting in a waiting room. It wasn't a doctor's surgery, but it was something similar. A few chairs and doors that go off into other rooms.

The place looked quite dreary and dark, it could have done with some light or some bright paint to make to feel a little happier. It seemed a dull place. I was told later it was CAMHS – a place where kids go to get diagnosed with things. That day, there was another boy in the waiting room. He was a similar age to me who was chatting about gaming to his dad. I loved gaming and began talking to the boy. I liked the boy. I liked the fact that we made friends – even if it was just for ten minutes. Looking back, I think he also had autism as he was very similar to me. Mum told me that we were going to see a doctor, the doctor wanted to do some puzzles and ask some questions. Mum told me that I had an amazing brain and that's why we were there. I was happy to go along though little did I know that this was part of my autism assessment. In the end, the lady doctor that saw me told me that I did have an amazing brain and not to let anyone ever tell me any different.

    A couple of days later mum and dad told me that I had something called Asperger syndrome which is a type of autism. They read a book to me about it. It was a kid's book that explained pretty much everything about how I felt. I nodded my head and said "Yes, that's just like me!" as mum cuddled up to me and smiled. We then watched a video, it was like a kid's video and I have to be honest the video did seem a bit silly. I wasn't digging the video but if it helped others understand autism a bit better then that's cool.

Mum and dad promised me that school would be better. They had told the school about my diagnosis and they thought school would understand me a bit better now.

Things did change a bit. I no longer was the last person in the classroom. When the school bell rang at 3.15 pm, I got to go out of a different exit. This was good as I didn't need to stand in the line looking at my mum through the glass in the door frame. We had our own special code back then. Mum would stand as close to the door as possible where she would brace herself as to whether we were in for another meeting or if we could just get home. I would do a thumbs up or a thumbs down depending on my day at school. As you probably guessed I pulled lots of sad faces and thumbs down through that window to mum. I remember even if it was a thumbs down mum would still smile back, I could see she was sad though. It made me sad that I had made her sad too, even if she was pretending to look ok. So now mum met me at a different exit, and we got home quicker!

The teachers even agreed to call mum during the day if there was a problem instead of us being held back. Maybe they could see mum's tired face? She was just as fed up as me listening to what I had done wrong. Mum told me that it wasn't me anymore that was being naughty or causing a problem, it was the teachers that weren't understanding me. Mum seemed more on my side now than ever. There was a big bonus of not staying behind, we got home quicker which means more time on my Xbox! Yes!

The children still seemed scared of me though, and mum tells me now that some of the parents from the school were complaining about me because I was disturbing the class during the day. I was unsure where they got that from because I was hardly ever in the classroom!? I kept being told to work outside with whoever was free in the corridor. It was suggested that my class friends watch a video on autism to understand me more. It was the same video that mum showed me in my bedroom. I was happy for them to do this, but I knew that it wouldn't make things any different. The children saw me as an angry person. One year, I found a Christmas card in my drawer and was excited that someone had been kind enough to send a Christmas card to me. When I opened it though it had a drawing of an angry face inside – I think that was meant to be me. Whoever sent it hadn't left their name in there either. I was really upset after that. Maybe I should have been happy that I got a card? I'm unsure? I think no card would have been better.

I was no longer forced to go into the assembly and could read a book in the quiet area. I was told I didn't even have to attend church because I hated church. I wasn't a big fan of the singing and I was a strong believer that when we leave this world that's just it. There isn't anything after - it just becomes black. Mum told me that we should respect everybody's religion and I think she is right. But I didn't like the way that I was being forced to go into church and I didn't like the vicar. Once he pushed me, so I hit him, he tried to hurry me up through the doorway. For one, I don't like being touched and for two, I hate being rushed. So, my church days ended quite quickly, but school listened to my mum and dad's request – they told them that it was more important to be happy during the day than have extra upset forcing me to take part in something that I hated. I'm also sure that they were worried that I may hit the vicar again.

The classroom set up changed. At first, I thought it was cool. I didn't have anyone kicking my chair leg to make me angry. I didn't have anyone stealing my pens. There were no excuses for the other children to get a reaction from me. I had my own space, though I was still finding things a little tricky. I am very clever - mum and dad tell me all the time, but now I know at the age of nine that I need my work to be broken up in small bits. Back then, I was given lots of instructions and my head couldn't take it all in. I wanted to keep up with everyone because I knew I could, but the teacher was just going way too fast. I would become frustrated and throw my pen across the room. I wouldn't hurt anyone, but the teachers always seemed to think that I was trying to.

This was when the teachers started removing me from the classroom. The teacher would look at me angry the same way as the scatty teacher in reception did (Mrs. Haribo face) This only made me angrier.

The way they removed me wasn't right, half the time the teaching assistant would grab me or pick me up and take me out of the classroom. As soon as this happened my class would start laughing. This just made me feel madder and sadder. Maybe if the teachers saw me struggling with my work, they could have given me the choice to spend some time outside of the classroom. Choices work but being forced to leave isn't going to work. It never did. It only made me fight. As soon as I started to fight back the adult in charge at the time would put pressure on me and it hurt. Imagine an adult's body weight compared to mine at the age of seven years old.

Even though mum and dad were speaking regularly to the teachers trying, to make adjustments throughout my day to make things easier - things just seemed to be getting worse. I was a kid that just wanted to be like the other kids, but instead, the kids in class saw me as the class clown. Most days felt like I had been thrown into a boxing ring fighting with staff.

Chapter 3 – Feeling Lonely

I'm sat on a desk just outside the classroom door. It's the beginning of a new day. I can hear all my class entering the room chatting and being generally happy, I wondered if they missed me being in the class with them or if they had even noticed? The desk has a little tray with toys in there, a fidget spinner, a stress ball and various other stuff for me to hold in my hands when things were getting tough. All these things at the time seemed cool but it wasn't helping me to feel any better. This time I was on my own outside. It was unpredictable which adult came and sat near me. I didn't want to do work any longer. I kept getting different people, some people would talk to me in a stern voice so I would react angrily. This would lead to me being grabbed and marched back to the headteacher's office.

The headteacher's office would be my next main location. I didn't like it there. It wasn't that it was a new scary place because since reception I knew it well. It was just the fact that I knew it was the next naughty place that I had to go.

In that office was a small table, a bookshelf and a couple of chairs. They were easy to grab as I knew what was coming. It was time for another round of Anthony Joshua back in the boxing ring.

Before they could grab me, I would run over to the bookshelf, grab a book and launch it at the wall. If I was super quick, I'd do a Sonic the Hedgehog move and spin past them and overturn the table. It all happened pretty fast, but their big bodies always won. I didn't have much chance of escaping in that small room. Although each time I managed to be able to find something new. At one point the headteacher was guarding his computer. I think he seriously thought I was going to launch that. I wasn't that strong although I was pretty strong for a seven-year-old if I do say so myself! Very soon the headmaster's office was pretty bare - they had managed to take most things out of there as they knew I was going to be a regular visitor.

My desk outside the classroom stayed there till the end of my school days at that school. I was isolated inside the school and even at lunch in my part of the playground.

Each morning mum and I would walk down the path through the school gates. The headteacher would be stood at the front of the school to greet the children. I didn't like to look at any of the staff. They pretended to be nice to me when mum was about but as soon as I was on my own, we would be in that boxing ring. I would get ready to hang my head as far as I could lowering it to my chest looking at the path to avoid eye contact - phew and we were past. Walking in hand with mum we carried on. Sometimes kids would be sniggering. Even mum noticed a few times and told me not to get angry and just ignore them. It was hard though. Why me?

We had our own section to stand in the playground in the morning. This was to allow us to get into class a few minutes earlier to avoid the stampede of my class barging me out of the way whilst I hung my coat and bag on the hanger. I noticed mum didn't talk to any of the parents anymore, mum put a brave face on and we would often make silly little games up in our section. Some days hopscotch and others just some crazy routines that mum had learned at the gym to keep us busy and moving. It made me happy.

When we got into the classroom I no longer wanted to learn, the happiness that I once had with mum drained out of me fast once I got into school. I didn't know who was going to be sat outside on my desk with me and most people who tried to work with me didn't come back. The teachers asked my mum what they should do as they said my day was spent doing pretty much nothing. I was tired, probably more than tired. I felt lonely, different and totally misunderstood. Most days a member of staff would restrain me, it hurt but I knew that I had to go to school each day because that's what everyone does. I am a big believer in doing what is right, but I knew everything that was happening wasn't right.

My parents knew things weren't right too, that I was being misunderstood, no one knew me or knew what to do with me. My mum and dad said that it was unacceptable and things needed to change.

Back at home, mum was chatting to dad about me being restrained a lot and how I was feeling so low; how I didn't want to do any work anymore and how things were affecting me. Mum didn't want me to go back to school, but dad worked at a law firm and knew the law and was worried. He said I needed to be in school, I heard mum shout at him. She doesn't often shout, but she told him that she didn't care about the law and we needed to sort something quickly with the school. Mum spent a lot of time on her computer on a night researching options for me. The options seemed quite simple. There was flexi-schooling. Flexi schooling is where I stayed at home with mum for a few days and did less time at school, or there was the option of just staying at home completely, or even moving to a different school. We decided on the first option. Let's do Monday, Tuesday and Wednesday at school and Thursday and Fridays at home. I did worry a little that I may miss certain things on the days that I was away from school but let's face it I was missing loads anyway sitting in the headteacher's office or outside in the corridor.

Chapter 4 - Part School Part Home

Mum had it all planned, she told me that she knew I was clever and wanted to learn but things just weren't right at school for me to do that. Mum had planned for me to start horse riding on a Thursday morning and on a Thursday afternoon we would go swimming. This sounded amazing. The swimming pool on a Saturday was difficult. The pool was busy and loud. Thursday was the only time the pool would be quieter. I would be able to concentrate more.

Horse riding was great too. I thought I was rubbish at everything at this point, but I wasn't. The horse was listening to me. I was listening to my instructor. At times I did worry that she was going to be like the teacher at school because she did seem a bit bossy, but I guess she had to be a little bossy as I was riding a horse this time and needed to listen. We started by going for a few walks down the woods. It was good; the instructor seemed to like me, she was kind and laughed at my jokes and listened to me. I enjoyed talking to her.

Was mum sure that we could do fun stuff? Would we get into trouble for doing fun things? I remember the teacher once saying that she didn't want me to think that I was just getting a long weekend (little did she know how much this was actually benefiting me.) I was listening to adults again, taking instructions. Mum was right - not all adults that teach are bad people that just want to restrain me or tell me what I am doing wrong. I was feeling good once again like I was able to do things. Completely the opposite of how I felt when I just gave up with everything sat at the school desk in the corridor.

To show the teachers how much my activities on a Thursday we're benefitting mc, we did written work for my book on a Friday which described everything I had done the day before.

I worried about writing at home because I had missed so much writing and spelling at school. I thought I might be a bit rubbish, I thought I would get frustrated, but I didn't. Mum chose some good work, things like Minecraft puzzle sheets for maths. We even did a cool project making a planet world and studied the moon and stars. I picked up a pen and wanted to write, although in pure panic mode I told mum I didn't have my pen license. Mum laughed and said we don't need to listen to that nonsense. "If you want to write with a pen you can write with a pen", she said. "If you want to hang upside down and write with a pen in the middle of your toes then that's fine too!", although that would have been impossible? There were no silly rules at home, and we made some great imaginary stories. Mum said I only needed to write 5 lines to start with, but whilst she wasn't looking, I filled the whole page! Mum's eyes were happy. I was happy and learning again.

We had breaks when I needed breaks, I could rest and then come back to work if my hands got tired. Mum never shouted or told me that I had to finish a task, we just went back to it when it was clearer in my mind.

We had a book that we took into school at the beginning of the week. The one I mentioned before - it was the "Friday book". We would stick all the work that I had completed at home inside it to show the teachers what we did at home. They never seemed that impressed but mum was really happy showing them. Maybe they wondered how we were achieving so much at home but when I was with them I didn't want to do anything. I was glad that I was making mum happy. I enjoyed doing work at home. But at school, it hadn't changed. Mum suggested the teachers should talk to me a little differently. Not to be so bossy with me and I would not get so angry but again, they didn't seem to listen.

Things at school got worse. I hated it but I didn't tell mum. I just put a brave face on and sat doing nothing. The teachers were asking my mum to give them ideas on what I would work on, but maybe it wasn't about the ideas. It was a whole different thing. That school wasn't right for me. No matter what different topics we could do I would still be told that I couldn't go into the class as I was a danger to the other children. They made me feel like an animal. None of the teachers really liked me, most rolled their eyes at me and would use the phrase "He's kicking off again" more times than ever instead of trying to understand the reason why. Just trying to understand me. Instead, it was just easier to hold me down, until I was too physically exhausted to do anything else all day.

Mum asked the school how they were coping and suggested that we may need to look at another school. The school agreed and said they would help us find the school that would make me happier. I think they just wanted to get rid of me. I still feel sad about that now. But I know what I have now is so much better as you will find out later in the story. I told you there were happier bits in it!

My parents sat me down and we had a good chat about what I wanted. I was given choices again, it was working well at home - me and mum, but I wanted school friends. I wanted to belong to a school. We just needed to find the right school that would understand me. Mum said there were schools out there that can help but it's not as simple as just finding one and starting there.

To get a different school I needed a document called an EHCP. By gosh this EHCP was tricky! It took mum and dad hours and hours to do. Actually, not hours it was months! Mum and dad pre-warned me that it wasn't just as simple as finding another school and moving, it would take time. But if I wanted this then they would fight hard to get it for me, but I had to be patient. I didn't realise how patient.

The weekends were boring. My dad had a busy job and mum was nagging him to do this important document. I wasn't sure what it was all about, I know it was about me and they wanted it to be just perfect so adults who worked with me in the future could understand me and we wouldn't have the same problems that we were having right now with school. It took a lot of time away from us as a family. Mum and dad were stressed, it started to make me feel sad.

The home wasn't a nice place. Dad couldn't spend time with me playing Minecraft. So, I was finding myself sitting in my room a lot on my own after a full day of being sat at school on my own. It was making me feel sad. This probably didn't help my mood when I went into school on the three days at the beginning of the week.

Mum and dad had enough, and so had I. Mum was concerned about the number of times I was being restrained and she told me that not all adults were like this. But in my eyes, the majority of adults that I had met were like this. The only few adults that I believe liked me now were at swimming or horse riding or my parents or my nana. I had lost all my trust in any of the other adults that worked with me or tried to work with me.

I was fed up with the way the teachers spoke to me. Always telling me what I can't do or that I shouldn't be doing something. It made me switch completely off. I felt like a computer; I had so much information in my head and wanted to go onto the next level. But now, I hit the power button and switched off completely. I sat for the last few weeks doing nothing, not talking to anyone and my arms firmly crossed.

One evening after school mum and dad sat down and spoke with me about what was going to happen the next morning at school. Was I going to suddenly start doing some work? The answer to that was probably no. Would I be sat in the headmasters' office all day? The answer to that was probably yes. Was there any point in going back to that school? The answer was no.

Chapter 5 – Good News

Mum told me that we had to go to the doctors. I had to go along and explain how school was making me sad and angry, although it was hard to explain to the doctor. All I knew was whilst I was at school, I felt sick, tired, angry, upset. Mum said I had high anxiety. I didn't want to sit and talk it all out again with the doctor. I had done this so many times with the teacher, but mum promised me this would be the last thing that I had to sit and listen to.

I went along and mum did most of the talking, the doctor said that he would send a letter to someone explaining my feelings and it was mum's decision on whether I should go into the school anymore. Mum told me I would never have to go back there again, so not to worry. All mum wanted was for me to be happy and not to worry about school for a long time. I felt relieved that I no longer needed to go back there but a little part of me was quite sad too. I had a few kids in my class that didn't laugh at me and were ok but there was a big majority that didn't want to be my friend. I was also a little bit worried about a new school. I don't think I'd be normal if I didn't worry. It's all change - and change is hard for me.

My mum and dad are the best. They booked a family holiday for us and we went to Disney in Florida. They knew that we hadn't been spending time together much and things had been really tough. At home me and mum planned out all sorts - our learning didn't just stop. We organised our holiday. It was fun. We worked out how many miles it was from each park. We figured out maps and even did maths by working out how long each ride lasted, and which rides we would go on, to plan out our day better.

I still noticed mum and dad working on that document even when we were on holiday, the document to get me into a different school came to Florida with us! But I was cool with that, at least we had fun during the day to be together. That holiday was amazing, and it did us all good to smile once again and enjoy life.

When we got home, mum found a good school that was around an hour's drive from us. We looked at the website and it explained that it had boys with Aspergers, PDA and ADHD. It also mentioned that it was for just boys who wanted to learn but would offer lots of help. It sounded perfect. I was happy but something always seems to go wrong. We found out I had to be nine years old to go there. Maybe I could wait at home till I was nine and then go? That was a long time away and mum and dad said I needed a new school sooner. The mission of finding the right school carried on.

Things seemed to stay quiet for a while - mum and dad were still messing around with this document.

It was a sunny fresh day in July when mum walked through the door and shouted for me to come down as she had something to tell me.

"Spencer! Spencer - you've been accepted at a new school!", she said excitedly.

I was shocked as I didn't know that there was another school that was going to be ok for me. I immediately felt happy - nearly as happy as it is when it's your birthday!

Mum opened her laptop up and started showing me the school. The school was a big school with lots of open fields around it. It had a farm - I loved animals! Mum also told me that there would only be nine children in my class and that we would have more staff helping us. It sounded perfect. Maybe I would get a friend there? Maybe people would like me there? I was excited. I told you we would get to some good parts, didn't I?

It was the summer holidays, so I had to wait five weeks before I started my new school. But in the meantime, we looked at the website a lot and the new headteacher told me that I could go and have a look around. There wouldn't be any pupils there as it was the holidays, but I was cool with that.

A friendly lady showed me around the school. It was bigger than I expected but the reason for this is because it is like a primary and secondary school all in one. The boys that go to my school are from ages seven to sixteen years old. I was excited and curious as we walked around. The school was very quiet with no children there, but I was happy to be returning in a few weeks to start for real. The lady told me that during the first week I could maybe do just a few afternoons and then the week after see how I felt. I replied quickly "No - that won't work. I must go full time straight away; I don't like change and if I do only half days in the first week the second week is going to be so much harder." The lady looked at me and smiled, my mum stroked my arm and smiled at me.

Chapter 6 – My New School

There were loads of changes at my new school and things I had to get used to. I have a house where I have leisure time, then I have a little school for younger kids like me. I am unsure how to act here? If I say that I don't want to do something are the teachers going to pounce on me or grab me by the arm and take me somewhere? I feel rather uneasy. It was easy to say that I wanted a new school but now I'm here I am getting nervous. The only way I show myself being nervous is by being angry.

The leisure time, in the beginning, went ok. There was an Xbox and the boys seemed to be ok. I was looking forward to break, I felt this area was going to be ok.

Next step they took me to the classroom, where the teacher and pupils were baking biscuits. The teacher asked me to take a seat and bake with them. Immediately it felt strange, I was now in a classroom and the teacher was asking me to work? I mean it was only baking, it was supposed to be fun right? But I didn't see it that way. When I heard the teacher tell me to take a seat and join in, I saw danger. I wondered what he would do if I told him that I didn't want to? So, I did just that. I was taken outside by one of the staff members and we went for a walk down the farm, this was a little better than going to the headmaster's office. I forgot all about the baking and the classroom and before we knew it, it was lunchtime. The dining area still felt pretty loud, but I managed to sit in there with the other boys. I was doing great considering that I hadn't had proper school dinners in a long time.

I started to shovel my peas and sweetcorn into my mouth using my hands just like I did when I was at home. The teacher wasn't too happy about my table manners and asked me to start using my knife and fork. I felt sad at this point. I had tried hard all day. It was my first day after all. I was also unsure about how to hold my knife and fork properly in my hands. Mum and dad let me use my fingers at home.

The last bit of the day we went to the house where we have breaks. I noticed that my class all had biscuits to take home, but I didn't get any. I chose not to take part, so I missed out. This made me feel sad. I love biscuits but I guess next time I must take part - it was my choice after all.

The boys were playing on the Xbox and invited me over to play, it felt good to be asked to join in. I was excited when we started playing a football game but one of the boys was sat close to me and by accident, my arm raised when I was close to scoring a goal. By accident, my arm hit his face. Before I knew it, I was flipped on my back and he was on top of me. One minute I had friends the next minute I was getting tackled. Was this the way they play here? It only happened for a second before I saw a member of staff hovering over me asking if I was ok. I was ok. I think I was ok? It might take getting used to, making friends here? I was so used to being the boy who would hit out at others. I had never been on the opposite side. That was a pretty quick learning lesson. I didn't like being hit, and the kids here certainly didn't like being hit either. I knew I wouldn't even try and hurt another pupil here, as I knew I would get it back.

I survived the first day. I was in one piece – but how I managed to hold back my tears until I jumped into the front seat of my mum's car I don't know. The minute she asked how my day went I burst into tears. I said it was terrible mum. I hated it. Mum cried too; I know she gets really upset when I am not happy. Mum said let's try another day and see how it goes.

Being me, I did just that, I wasn't going to let my first day put me off. I was made of stronger sweetcorn and peas than you will ever think.

The next day me and the boy who pinned me to the floor over the Xbox game did some baking together, we got on well. I soon figured that he was just like me at my old school. We were so used to going into the boxing ring with adults and other kids I guess it was hard to know that we were safe now. This kind of stuff still goes on, but mum says I have figured it out a bit quicker than some of the other boys because I am very clever. My second day went a bit better, and each day got easier. The teachers listen to me; the teachers want to be my friend. My class teacher is amazing - she allows us to walk out of the room when I am feeling a little anxious. She also created a "beef bunker" under her desk. This isn't the beef you eat, it's when another kid in the class is showing a bit of attitude. It's a safe place where you can go to let it all out. How cool is that? I also have a one to one support worker; I sometimes don't need their help but it's good to have someone next to you if you're finding things tricky.

Then there is my amazing key worker Georgie! She gets me and listens to me. She is another adult friend that has my back at school. We had lots of fun last year; we had a school day out at a theme park. Georgie hates rollercoasters but as she was my key worker, she had to come on all of them with me. I think she looked pretty green at the end of the day.

I enjoy reading, the school are amazed by my reading, they love me to read so often I volunteer to read anything in assembly. Can you remember when I hated assemblies? I hated them because I felt different. I was pointed at, had to sit by the side of a teacher or be marched out.

I no longer feel different at this school. I soon realised that there are lots of kids that struggle like me and just need understanding, but I talk about that more in the last chapter.

So back to school - yes, it's not always easy. I would be lying if I said that every day was perfect. But it's a massive change compared to when I used to get held every day.

When I wasn't allowed next to the other kids.

When I had to sit outside of the classroom all day.

I do fun stuff. The mission is to learn but not make me angry. It's sometimes a little tricky as we have boys in the class who are struggling and when they are it makes it hard to concentrate. But we have a lot of good times. Recently the teacher has noticed I struggle with the disruption. I now have my own partition on my desk so I can concentrate on my work. It's personalised too with photos of sloths because I love sloths! I also have some ear defenders with an mp3 player that plays my favourite music. How amazing is that! Now I no longer spend much time being disturbed and can just get on with my work.

I've been away with school twice now; at my old school, I wasn't even allowed on a school trip without my mum. The school had to do a risk assessment on me. If mum couldn't come, then I wasn't allowed to go on day trips.

On the first trip at my new school, we stayed away for a whole week at Butlins. I wasn't scared but my mum was nervous. Mum was worried that I would miss home as

I hadn't slept away before. Mum kept prompting me to just call her if I needed collecting, but I was having the time of my life. When we got back to school, I got an award for being the best boy at camp! With it being my first time away from home to be told that, well, it made me feel wonderful.

Then the second time I went away for four nights. We did challenges like rafting and rock climbing - things that I never thought I could do. I was made to feel like I couldn't do anything at my old school. Made to feel very strange and useless. Here I was feeling like I could achieve so much … and I was going to achieve more!

Chapter 7 – Friends

My first year at school went well. There were a few wobbly moments, but I guess nothing is perfect. More importantly, there were two boys that I became really good friends with. They were very similar to me, both liked gaming and they were both kind. We all worked well in our group. I had my own little team. It still makes me sad thinking of the good times though. Because the boys were a little older than me, the next year they got moved up a class. But I had friends. I still see them in school at lunch, but I wish I could see them more. It still makes me sad to talk about this, because I had never in my whole life had real friends until then. I still cry a little thinking of this bit, but I get on with things. I have to I guess. Sometimes things are out of your control. Even my mum and dad couldn't sort this one out. If only I was a few years older I could have moved up too. But I am not, and I have to just get on with this fact.

Friends can be tricky at a specialist

school. You see, we all have our own little problems. Some days the kids with ADHD can be a little too bouncy for me. I can find that irritating, then some boys just come to school and struggle to get on with their work so they might get angry. This can upset me as I don't like loud noises. I guess we are all at a specialist school for a reason. We all have our little problems. I'm not an angel either. I can get upset quickly if someone says something as a joke. Sometimes, I don't realise it's a joke and I read it a different way. My autism sometimes makes my mind think differently from others. I also don't like it if a teacher uses a stern voice, so that can make me walk off. If someone I don't know well touches me, or leads me, or pushes me that can make me angry. It kind of reminds me of being led away so many times at my old school. So, you get the idea here - we all have our moments. It's not that the boys are all nasty or mean. They're not. They just have other stuff going on, but sometimes it isn't easy at a school like mine. Let's say it can be a little unpredictable. But when it's good it's good! When most of the boys are having a good day then it's a great day here.

    Just recently though I mentioned to mum that I am grateful that I do have friends at school, but it would be nice to have other friends, friends that don't swear as much. At an all-boys school, you can't get away from the boys that swear, most do it. I even find myself doing it now and again to just fit in and be a boy there. But I don't like it. I think at any school kids swear, a mainstream school or a specialist school - it's just part of life. Even mum and dad do if they're angry about something, but it doesn't often happen at home. Mum says that people who swear don't know how to speak properly and that's why they can only use bad language. Life is better without swearing and anger.

Getting back to the point – I don't often see my friends that moved up a class and my class friends can be a little unpredictable at times.

I just crave to meet friends that understand me. I find myself a very understanding kid. I never used to be able to understand others but as I am getting older it's easier to do. For example, one boy at school can be a little annoying but when he apologises to me, I forgive him as I know it's not easy for that kid to say sorry. So, I try and understand. I also understand when other kids at school are finding things tough and then maybe shout out. I used to do that when I had high anxiety. I get that. But I don't think that any kids in my class understand me. They're too busy trying to understand themselves! Finding a friend that understands me would be cool.

I have a few cool lad mates, but they have PDA. Pathological Demand Avoidance - it's what I have too. If ask them to come over for tea one night or just have a play day it can never be arranged too far in advance as it depends on how they're feeling that day. PDA can sometimes suck! But again, I understand that it isn't my friend's fault. See I am super understanding.

This brings me to the Facebook group that my mum runs. When we started flexi-schooling a long time ago, mum wanted to document everything that we had been doing just in case anyone from the local authority needed proof that we were learning things every day.

Mum's Facebook page has been pretty good actually. She has a lot of mums that join, and they all talk to each other and support each other with putting up with kids like us! Although I think it should be the other way around - but mum might go mad if I say that. Never mind it had to be said. On a positive note, mum has met some nice people through her group. People that have kids like me that can come and play online with me, they have helped. I've met friends that don't even go to school and are home-schooled. I have to say my home school friends online are a lot more chilled out and don't swear.

I tried a local boys street dance club in my area. It was ok but the kids there didn't want to learn and spent the whole hour not following instructions and being told off. It reminded me a little bit of school. I wanted a hobby that made me smile - not remind me of how my day had been at school, so I decided to give this up.

I recently joined a local arts club. I enjoy the club, the only thing is the group is all girls, the only boy that went has now dropped out which was a shame. I hope a boy joins up soon. I don't mind the girls, but I could do with a lad there for a bit of lad chat.

So, as you can see for a kid that isn't too fussed on socialising, I don't do bad, do I?

Chapter 9

At the start of the book, it was tough. I was isolated away from everyone because I wasn't understood. I was classed as a naughty boy that just enjoyed going around smacking other kids and then being laughed at, stared at, pointed at. Which kid honestly would enjoy that or want to feel like that? Thank goodness my mum and dad listened to me otherwise I would hate to think how I would have been feeling right now. Still in my little section of the playground and sat in the corridor or sat next to the headteacher in his room.

Luckily, moving to a specialist school with other kids that had worries and were upset made me see that I wasn't bad after all. I wasn't the only kid out there that was feeling this way. There were other kids just like me. The minute that I could see that I was no longer the only frustrated angry boy in this world I wanted to help the other boys that felt this way.

I understood that maybe the boys

wouldn't want to be my friend straight away, it might take time for them to see that I was kind, but maybe they didn't know how I was going to react because they hadn't had real friends either?

    I have learned that when I see another child kicking, screaming or sounding angry I don't laugh or snigger or whisper. I understand that that kid is struggling. I know how that feels. It's not nice. People need to understand that.

    I wish other people understood me. We can all be different, but we might have reasons why we are different and if people choose to accept that, then the world would be a much better place.

    Thank you for reading my story. I hope it has helped you to feel like you're not different or odd or strange.

You're unique. You're gifted;

And, if we ever meet, I will understand you.

Spencer
11th March 2020

For parents and carers:

If your child has special needs and you are struggling to get the support you need, Spencer's mum, Katie, has also written a book.

Katie details how she fought for the support that Spencer needed and eventually managed to secure him a place in a special school. Katie details the legal process and how she dealt with many of the challenges she faced.

An honest and open account, Katie hopes to help others going through similar situations.

Life on an Alien Planet is available now on Amazon.

Printed in Great Britain
by Amazon